Snake

🔗 **Dominie Press, Inc.**

Snake has eyes,
but it cannot see well.
Snake has a nose,
but it cannot smell well.

Snake's tongue can feel
movement in the air.
Snake's tongue can sense smells.

Snake's tongue helps
its eyes and nose.

What can that hungry snake feel and taste with its tongue?

A little bird!

Snake slides closer and closer.

Be careful, little bird!

**Oh, good!
The little bird got away.**